LIVEWIRE
REAL LIVES

# Chelsea

**the information store** ☎01603 773114
email: tis@ccn.ac.uk

**21 DAY LOAN**

Published in association with The Basic Skills Agency

# Hodder & Stoughton

A MEMBER OF THE HODDER HEADLINE GROUP

**Acknowledgements**

*Photos: pp. iv, 15, 19, 25 © Action-Plus Photographic,*
*pp. 3, 11, 22 © Action Images, p. 7 © Popperfoto.*
*Cover photo: © Allsport.*

Orders: please contact Bookpoint Ltd, 39 Milton Park, Abingdon, Oxon OX14 4TD. Telephone: (44) 01235 400414, Fax: (44) 01235 400454. Lines are open from 9.00–6.00, Monday to Saturday, with a 24 hour message answering service. Email address: orders@bookpoint.co.uk

*British Library Cataloguing in Publication Data*
A catalogue record for this title is available from The British Library

ISBN 0 340 71164 7

First published 1998
Impression number 10 9 8 7 6 5 4 3 2
Year 2002 2001 2000 1999

Typeset by Fakenham Photosetting Ltd, Fakenham, Norfolk.
Printed in Great Britain for Hodder & Stoughton Educational, a division of Hodder Headline Plc, 338 Euston Road, London NW1 3BH by Redwood Books, Trowbridge, Wiltshire.

# Contents

If you want style,
come to Chelsea.

If you want class,
and classy football,
come to Chelsea.

If you want to see world-class football stars,
the best that money can buy,
you will find them at Stamford Bridge.

If you want thrills and football skills,
and all-round entertainment,
come to Chelsea Football Club!

# 1 History

Before there was a Chelsea Football Club,
there was a Stamford Bridge.
It was a stadium for athletics.

Fulham FC had the chance
to move to Stamford Bridge.
But they said no.
They wanted to stay at their ground,
Craven Cottage.

So some players got together
at Stamford Bridge
and made a team.

They called it Chelsea Football Club.
That was in 1904.

So Chelsea were late starters.

At first, they were often in the shadow
of older London clubs.
Clubs like Spurs or Arsenal
had been around longer than Chelsea.

Stamford Bridge – Chelsea FC's football ground.

Things started well for Chelsea.
In their very first season,
they scored 90 goals in just 38 games.
That's still the club record.

Right from the start,
Chelsea had an image.

They were the stylish boys
of London's trendy King's Road.
They had class.
They had money.
They bought skilful players.

But they never won anything.
Not until 50 years later – in 1955!
(They won the League
for the one and only time!)

But they did come close in 1915.
They were in the FA Cup Final.
But lost to Sheffield United.

And they had to spend some time
in the 2nd Division
when things didn't go so well.

# 2 Stars and Legends

Jimmy Greaves was a brilliant player.

He was so fast on the ball.
And he could dribble through any defence.
He didn't have a powerful shot.
He just seemed to walk the ball
past defenders and into the net.

Everyone remembers Greaves
as a Spurs player.
Everyone forgets he played for Chelsea too.
In fact,
Chelsea was his first club (1957–61).

In 1960–61,
he scored 41 goals for Chelsea
in the League.
That's still the club record.

And he scored his first 100 League goals
while he was a Chelsea player.
He was still only 20 at the time.

Chelsea's first world-class side
came together around 1969–70.
The manager was Dave Sexton.
Every player was a character.
Every player was a star.

There was goal keeper Peter Bonetti
(known as 'The Cat').

There was Ron Harris.
He was known as 'Chopper'.
He was the hard man of the defence.
The best tackler in the game.
(Someone once said:
'If Ron Harris was in a good mood,
he would put disinfectant on his studs
before he tackled you!')

And up front there were
Charlie Cooke, Peter Osgood
and Alan Hudson.

That team won the FA Cup in 1970.
Peter Osgood scored in every round.
Next year, they won the Charity Shield,
and the European Cup Winners' Cup.

It has taken over 25 years
for Chelsea to build a team that good.

Ron Harris lifts the 1970 FA Cup.

Why did it take so long?

Chelsea Chairman Ken Bates
thinks he knows why.
He has some harsh words
for the stars of the 1970s.
He says they helped to sink the club
for 20 years.

'They were just Jack-the-Lads,'
says Ken.
'They didn't train.
They didn't want to learn
or to get better.
They just thought it was all about having a laugh.
Having a good time.'

Winning came so easy,
so they stopped trying.

Then the younger players
stopped trying as well.
They thought it would be easy.

It took 20 years to stop the rot.

# 3 Famous Fans

Chelsea has always had famous fans.
People like John Major,
the last Tory Prime Minister.
(Though he likes cricket more than football.)
And another MP: Tony Banks.
He is Minister for Sport.

In May 1997,
Tony Banks went to the FA Cup Final.
But he didn't want to sit in the Royal Box
like a Minister for Sport should.
He went and sat with his mates.
Just like he did every Saturday.

'I just want to enjoy the game,' he said.
'I don't want to sit there with a straight face,
I want to have a really good time!'

Then there are other famous fans:
Singer and TV presenter, Suggs.
David Baddiel, the presenter
of TV's Fantasy Football.
And 'Blur' singer, Damon Albarn.

These people know a class act
when they see one!

# 4 Matthew Harding

Perhaps Chelsea's biggest and best fan
was Matthew Harding.
He was a millionaire business man.
He loved Chelsea FC.
He poured millions of pounds into the club.

He was Vice Chairman of the club.
Sometimes he didn't see eye-to-eye
with Ken Bates, the Chairman.

Ken Bates wanted to build a new stadium
at Stamford Bridge.
The Chelsea of the future.
Matthew Harding wanted to build a new team,
just as classy and successful
as the stars of 1970.

In the end,
Matthew Harding and Ken Bates did both.
They built a brilliant new stadium
and a brilliant new team!
But it cost millions of pounds
of Matthew Harding's money.

Ken Bates (left) and Matthew Harding (right).

In October 1996,
Matthew Harding and three friends
set off in his helicopter.

They were off to see a football match.
But the helicopter crashed
soon after take-off.

Everyone on board was killed.
Matthew Harding was 42 years old.

Everyone in football went into mourning.

The leader of the Labour Party,
Tony Blair,
went to Matthew's funeral.
(Matthew had just given £1 million
to the Labour Party.)

Chelsea stars old and new –
Peter Osgood, Dave Webb, Ruud Gullit
and Gianluca Vialli
– all came to pay their respects.
For Chelsea fans, it felt like
they had lost a member of the family.

One day,
a newspaper had asked Matthew Harding
what dreams he had for the year 2000.

He had three:
Tony Blair would be in Downing Street;
England (under ex-Chelsea manager Glenn Hoddle)
would win the European Championships;
and Chelsea would win the Premier League.

One of these dreams
has already happened!

But sadly,
Matthew Harding didn't live long enough
to see any of his dreams come true.

# 5 Ruud Gullit

Ruud Gullit was born on 1 September 1962.
He grew up in Amsterdam
in Holland.

His mother was Dutch.
His father was from Surinam.
Surinam had been a Dutch colony
in South America.

He was once in a reggae band;
they had a hit in the charts in Holland!

He was captain of the Dutch team
in the late 1980s.

But he played his best football
in Italy.
He played for AC Milan (twice)
and Sampdoria (twice).

Ruud Gullit.

He won the European Cup
with Milan in 1989.
Milan beat Dan Petrescu's side
(from Romania).
The score was 4–0,
and Ruud scored two goals.

He was European Player of the year
in 1987.

Chelsea manager Glenn Hoddle
brought him to London in 1995.
It was the right time for Chelsea.
And it was the right time for Ruud.

He was getting injured all the time
in Italy.
Chelsea were also keen
to build a new international team
round their new international star.

Ruud really enjoyed himself
in English football.

After Ruud had been here a year
– in 1996 –
manager Glenn Hoddle left Chelsea.
He went on to be England manager.

Ruud became Chelsea manager.
He got no pay rise in his new job.
But then he *was* getting over £1 million a year
as a player!

At first,
it wasn't easy for Ruud to make changes.

He wasn't a player any more.
And the players weren't team-mates any more.

But Ruud knew what he wanted.
And he wasn't scared
of upsetting people.

Some players fell out
and left the club.

But Ruud knew what he had to do.
He sacked the trendy diet experts,
and the aroma-therapy experts.

Instead, he made
the players train twice a day.

# 6 Chelsea International

The famous Chelsea side of 1970
was all British.
One or two Scots, the rest English.

But the team that Ruud Gullit built
in 1996–97
was truly international.

Apart from home-grown talents,
there were players from Russia,
Norway, Romania, France and Italy.

It is easy for Chelsea
to attract international stars.
Chelsea is in London,
and London is full of life, full of fun.

This is one big attraction
for the rich young footballers
who come to play in this country.

The 1997 Chelsea squad.

As one player said:
'I always looked up to Ruud.
He was like someone from another planet.
When I heard he wanted me
to play for Chelsea,
I was amazed he had even heard of me!'

And a lot of big name players
wanted to come to Chelsea.
Just so they could play for Ruud.

# 7 That Cup Final

'This Cup Final is as important to me
as the European Cup Final
I won with Milan,'
said Ruud Gullit.

The 1997 FA Cup Final was to be
his first big final as a manager.
In fact,
that Final was famous for a lot of 'firsts'.

Ruud was the first foreign manager
– and the first black manager –
to take a team to Wembley.
He was also the first to win.
Chelsea beat Middlesbrough 2–0.

Mark Hughes won his 4th Cup Winner's Medal.
That was a first too.

But the best record-breaker
was Chelsea's opening goal.

Roberto di Matteo scored
after only 43 seconds.
The quickest ever at a Wembley final!

Roberto di Matteo scores in the FA Cup Final, 1997.

Chelsea captain Dennis Wise
won the ball from Middlesbrough
straight from the kick-off.

He passed to Roberto di Matteo
inside the Chelsea half.
The Italian just ran up the field
and let fly from 25 metres.

He caught the keeper off his line.
But the shot was already unstoppable.
The ball flew into the net
off the under-side of the bar.

After a start like that,
Middlesbrough never got into the match.
Chelsea out-played them all afternoon.

Eddie Newton sealed it for Chelsea
ten minutes from time.
It was Chelsea's first big win for 26 years.

The fans were singing and cheering.
The players were dancing all over the pitch.

But Ruud was calm and cool:
'We did what we had to do,' he said.
'Everybody did their job.'

But Ruud did say he was happy as well:
'I am happy for Ken Bates,' he said.
'And I am happy for Matthew Harding.
He died last year.
But really,
he has been with us all season.
It's like he has been a part of us.'

But then it was back to business:
'Now we can have a holiday.
We deserve it.
But when we get back,
we must start thinking about next year.
And the future.'
But little did Ruud know
that he would miss out on the future!
He was sacked on 12 February 1998.

Dennis Wise holds up the 1997 FA Cup.

Chelsea wing-back, Dan Petrescu
sums up Chelsea's game:

'At Chelsea,' he says,
'you will always see chances.
You will always see some goals.
It is hard to see Chelsea drawing 0–0!'
This is just like the great teams of old.
It's how Chelsea will always play.

Chelsea fans will be hoping –
– that the defence gets tighter;
– that the forwards keep on scoring;
– that the football gets even more exciting;
– and that the trophies keep coming home
  to Stamford Bridge!